THE HUNTERS AND THE ELK

BY KARA RACE-MOORE

ILLUSTRATIONS BY JERRY TIRITILLI

Scott Foresman
is an imprint of

Glenview, Illinois • Boston, Massachusetts • Chandler, Arizona
Upper Saddle River, New Jersey

Every effort has been made to secure permission and provide appropriate credit for photographic material. The publisher deeply regrets any omission and pledges to correct errors called to its attention in subsequent editions.

Unless otherwise acknowledged, all photographs are the property of Pearson.

Photo locations denoted as follows: Top (T), Center (C), Bottom (B), Left (L), Right (R), Background (Bkgd)

Illustrations by Jerry Tiritilli

Photographs 12(c) Dorling Kindersley

ISBN 13: 978-0-328-51386-4
ISBN 10:   0-328-51386-5

9 10 VOFL 16 15 14 13

The Snohomish people still live in what is now Washington State. They have lived there for a long time. They were known for hunting elk. The elk gave them meat for food. They made clothing from elk skin. They made tools, weapons, and art from elk antlers.

The elk were very important to the Snohomish. Elk even became part of a constellation. This tale tells how that happened. It explains what the Snohomish saw overhead in the night sky. It also honors the elk that they hunted.

The Snohomish say the Creator went from east to west. As he went he made the land. He gave people different languages. The languages let the people speak.

The Creator stopped when he reached the land of the Snohomish. There he left his leftover languages.

There were too many languages! No one could understand anyone. The people were unhappy.

They were unhappy for other things. The Creator had not made the sky high enough. People bumped their heads on the stars. The sky was not easy to get around either.

The people got together. They agreed to push up the sky. But none of them spoke the same language! One leader asked, "How will we know when to push?"

"We can use a word as a signal to start pushing," said another leader. They decided on the word *ya-hoh*. It would mean "lift together!"

The leaders explained the plan. People made poles out of tall trees. When the signal was given, they would push and poke the sky up with their poles.

When the people heard *ya-hoh*, they pushed and poked at the sky. They pushed as hard as they could. They lifted the sky!

   While everyone else was pushing,
three hunters were chasing four elk. These
hunters had been away while the plan had
been explained.
   Just when the pushing started, the four
elk reached a place where the sky touched
the earth. The elk raced into the sky. The
hunters followed!

The elk and the hunters wanted to return from the sky. It was too late! They became trapped in the sky. After a while they turned into seven stars.

People call these seven stars the Big Dipper. During the year, the hunters seem to move. In the fall the hunters are low in the sky. They seem to touch the ground.

Now, when people work together, they still shout "ya-hoh!" or "heave-ho!" People shout it when they need everyone to put their strength into a hard task.

When people work together they can do great things. That is the lesson of the Snohomish story.

Constellations

The stars in the sky seem to move when you look at them. They seem to move because the Earth moves around the Sun.

Have you ever heard a narrator tell stories about constellations? People make constellations by drawing imaginary lines between stars.

For thousands of years, people have imagined stories about the stars. The Big Dipper is a set of stars. It is part of another constellation. It has many names and stories. The Snohomish people call it the Elk Hunters.